How To Make Money

In Japan

HOW TO MAKE MONEY
IN JAPAN

by DOMENICO LAGANA

YOHAN PUBLICATIONS, INC.

Tokyo, Japan

HOW TO MAKE MONEY IN JAPAN

A YOHAN LOTUS BOOK/Published 1989
2nd printing October 1991

Cover design by Domenico Lagana

YOHAN PUBLICATIONS, INC.

14-9 Okubo 3-chome, Shinjuku-ku, Tokyo, Japan

Printed in Japan

PREFACE

In writing this book, I have drawn information from the contributions to a special readers' column which was published in the *Asahi Shimbun* from September 1, 1988 to January 9, 1989 and from March 1, 1989 to June 30, 1989. It was entitled *Okane* (Money), and readers were invited to write about their personal experiences and way of thinking about financial matters, taxation, land prices, social welfare, corporations, and the connection between money and politics in Japan.

I have also drawn facts and interpretations from the writings of journalists, columnists and readers of *The Japan Times* and some other newspapers and magazines.

I wish to thank Mr. Michio Nagasawa, of the Editorial Staff of the *Asahi Shimbun,* for his kind cooperation in supplying me with the necessary newspaper cuttings, and express my indebtedness to the writers of the letters and articles which I have summarized or referred to.

Contributions to the readers' column *Okane* reached a total of 795. The Publication Department of the *Asahi Shimbun* has edited a selection entitled *Okane—Nihonjin no Kinsenkan* (Money: The Japanese Attitude), which has recently been published by Asahi Shimbunsha.

The selection contains 530 contributions, which give a vivid description of the peculiarities and paradoxes in contemporary Japanese society. It is an extremely interesting book, and I hope that it will be translated.

CONTENTS

1

THE LAND OF IDEALISTS
WHO DESPISE MONEY

About a year and a half ago I got into conversation with a man sitting at the next table in a restaurant. He said that he was an American columnist, and had just come to Japan in order to gather material for a series of articles on life in Japan.

He asked me how long I had been in this country, and whether I liked it. I told him that I had been living in Japan for more than 13 years, and I liked it here so much that I had no intention of going back to my home country.

"Are you a businessman?"

"No. I'm a university professor."

"I see. Did you come to Japan at the invitation of the university?"

"Not when I came for the first time. It's a long and complicated story, and I will not bore you

with it. When I first visited Japan, more than 15 years ago, I felt an irresistible attraction to the Japanese way of life, and after overcoming a lot of obstacles, my dream of settling down in Japan at last came true."

"Why did you feel such an attraction?"

I answered that when I first came to Japan, I felt as if after many long years of living in a materialistic world, I had at last found an idyllic country of idealistic people who looked upon money as a secondary thing in life.

He stared at me, as if wondering whether I was pulling his leg. But then he seemed to realize that I was speaking in earnest, and asked me if I still believed that they were such idealists.

I said that since Japan has become a great economic power, the Japanese way of life has undergone great changes, and it was impossible for me to generalize.

"All I can tell you is that my circle of acquaintances is not very large, but my Japanese friends are all the same kind of people as I met when I first came to Japan."

He again stared at me, drank up his coffee, and after wishing me good luck, he went to pay his bill. When he was walking towards the door, he looked back at me with a puzzled expression, and smiled.

I think that I left him with the impression that I was an old fool who was living in an ivory tower.

2

THE WONDERLAND OF POLITICIANS

I do not know whether I am a fool, but it is a fact that since I came to Japan until recently I was living in an ivory tower.

But not my wife. Although she is not Japanese, like a model Japanese wife, she holds the purse strings, and has always been in close touch with reality. And of course, she has always been complaining about the high cost of living, the rent that increases every two years, the educational expenses of our son, and the oppressive taxes that prevent any attempt at saving money.

The Recruit affair and the consumption tax were the last straw.

Every day she read the English-language newspaper from cover to cover, and the topic of conversation at breakfast, lunch and dinner changed from money to politics, or to be more exact, from our lack of money to the abundance of it in the pockets of the politicians involved in the scandal.

It was true that the Recruit affair was revealing a political corruption which was beyond words. It was also true that the only object of the consumption tax seemed to be contributing a few more trillion yen for the activity of Japanese politicians at home, and the prosperity of Japanese corporations at home and overseas. But we could not do anything to change the situation, and instead of talking all the time about it, wasn't it better to ignore it, and let matters take their own course?

After reading the headlines of the newspaper and glancing through the articles which excited her indignation, I tried to change the topic by making jokes, but it was no use. She went on grumbling, and I just listened and nodded until she decided to put an end to her monologue by saying that she simply could not understand why the people of Japan were allowing all that to happen.

"They just don't care, do they?"

I did not think that they were indifferent, but foreigners who do not know the psychological structure of the Japanese people were all getting the same impression as my wife.

The problem is that the Japanese psychological structure is so different from ours, and so complicated, that it is practically impossible to understand it perfectly.

If you master the language, have read hundreds of books of all kinds in the original, and have been living here for many years, you may succeed, but not necessarily.

According to an article by Fred Hiatt, which was published in *The Japan Times* on June 25, 1989, there are people of pure Japanese heritage, born and bred in Japan, who after living in America for a number of years, come back to Japan and fail to understand the mentality of their own fellow countrymen.

The article is about a 49-year-old naturalized American citizen who was born in Japan, attended college here and went to the United States at 24, after getting a Japanese master's degree.

Some time ago he came to Japan with a high-tech product to sell, a multi-billion corporation to back him up and a partnership with some blue-chip Japanese companies.

No one could complain that he did not know the language and the customs. He failed miserably, and was forced to retreat, a beaten and embittered man.

"I was born in Japan, I was brought up in Japan, but I still don't understand it," he said.

It sounds like a joke, but it isn't.

3

THE INSCRUTABLE
JAPANESE MIND

If you are a Japanologist, and have reached the stage where you can flatter yourself that you understand the Japanese way of thinking, when you try to explain it to your fellow countrymen, you will be surprised to see that it is as difficult for them to understand you as it was for you to understand the Japanese when you first came into contact with them.

That is why books about Japan, even if they are written by eminent Japanologists, nearly always fail to give a convincing image of Japan, which still defies efforts at internationalization, and is as "inscrutable" as ever.

In a contribution to the readers'column of the *Asahi Shimbun* entitled *Okane* (Money), dated September 24, 1988, a 21-year-old Japanese girl student wrote about a foreign acquaintance of hers, who was complaining about Japan.

"The longer I live in this country, and the less I understand it. I have the impression that what is happening is sheer madness. Are the Japanese resigned to their fate? Have they become insensitive? Are they tolerating it because they have no other option? Really, I don't know what to think. By the way, are you indifferent too?"

"It's not that I am indifferent. But I have no idea what we should do. The whole society is like an enormous ghost."

He was silent for a while, and then he said, in broken Japanese, what the naturalized American citizen born and bred in Japan who failed to understand his fellow countrymen thought in perfect Japanese and probably expressed in English with a slight Japanese accent.

"It's no use. I don't understand Japan."

I have been in Japan much longer than her friend, and until the incredible corruption of a great number of Japanese politicians came to light, I was under the delusion that I understood Japan and the Japanese.

But when I came out of my ivory tower, and began to read newspapers and magazines, which were full of articles about the indignant reaction of the Japanese people, while nothing was happening that might corroborate it, I reached the same conclusion : I couldn't make head or tail of it.

Have the Japanese people become insensitive, or are they leading such a good life that they couldn't care less?

Although I do not know exactly what this girl meant by "enormous ghost," I suppose that she was trying to say that the common people were quite helpless, and could not even try to fight against the powerful political party that has been dominating Japan since the end of the war.

It is difficult to imagine that in a really critical situation brought about by the corruption of the ruling party, the people of any country in the world would feel as impotent as the Japanese appeared to do.

One possible explanation would have been that thanks to that political party, they are leading such a comfortable life, that they could well afford to forget the whole thing after grumbling about the lack of ethics of politicians and so forth. Are they leading such a life?

On the other hand, judging from the reaction on the part of the politicians involved in the scandal, who were behaving as if the whole affair were nothing to worry about, and defending themselves in a way that would have delighted the audience of a European or

American comedian, it was impossible to imagine that the Japanese people were so gullible as to believe what they were saying.

And unless the working people of Japan, who did not even declare a protest strike when the same politicians railroaded the consumption tax, are earning salaries that would not be affected by it, it was hard to understand why they did not even try and refuse to pay it when it was imposed in a way which in the mass media was described as arrogant, insolent and shameless. Are they earning such fat salaries?

4

LIFE IN THE LAND OF MAMMON

According to Japanese journalists and columnists, although there are relatively few people who are making huge fortunes at one stroke and wallowing in luxury, the great majority of the working class are struggling to make both ends meet on a meager salary.

Does such description reflect the real situation? I am not in a position to express an opinion based upon my own experience.

The Japanese people with whom I am in contact do not belong to either of these two categories. Almost all of them are university professors, and although they are much better off than I am, they are definitely not leading a life of luxury. Therefore, I cannot say that I personally know any rich Japanese people.

There are some young lecturers or assistant professors who sometimes complain about the cost of living, and the impossibility of buying a house or an apartment, but they are not in a really bad economic situation. Therefore, I cannot say either that I am personally acquainted with any Japanese people who, by European or American standards, might be described as poor.

I have also heard and read that in the last few years the Japanese way of thinking about money matters has changed radically, and that Japan has become the Land of Mammon, where the only object in life is making money.

About this, too, I must admit my ignorance, for I have never been in close contact with any Japanese "money-worshippers" who are talking all the time about their Almighty God.

As a matter of fact, I got the chance of coming to Japan thanks to the kind assistance and cooperation of Japanese intellectuals who never spoke about money, as if it were the least important thing in life. And all the people with whom I got acquainted when I came here were very delicate about topics connected with money.

That is why when the American columnist asked my opinion about the Japanese, I answered in a way which contradicted what he had heard about "economic animals," and he reacted as if I were mentally deranged.

On the other hand, I did not settle down in Japan either to make money or to analyze the ideology of the Japanese people as regards money, but in order to improve my knowledge of the Japanese language, which I had learned to read and write by myself, and live among people to whom I felt attracted.

Since I came to Japan, I have written a large number of essays, articles, columns and serials in the most important Japanese newspapers and magazines, and have published nine books in Japanese, including a novel about Italy which was given favorable reviews by literary critics.

Nowadays in Japan there are not only the "haves" and "have nots," but also those who "are believed to have"—and I am one of these. For all my Western friends and acquaintances believe that thanks to my writings, I have amassed a fortune of billions of yen. And for instance, they often ask me how much I paid for "my" house, although I have told them hundreds of times that it is not mine, and that with all the increases in the last few years, the rent has become a severe burden.

The truth is that although my literary activity has transformed me into the Italian version of a Japanese workaholic, and as incurable as all of them are, I have accumulated as much money as many of them do : almost zero.

And as I have been too busy teaching, writing and pursuing my study of contrastive linguistics, I have left my wife in charge of money matters, thus losing touch with the practical realities of life.

The Recruit affair and the consumption tax, and the reaction of my wife, obliged me to get out of my ivory tower. And I began to do what I had never done : read newspapers and magazines instead of novels, theses and monographs.

It was thanks to the readers' column *Okane* of the *Asahi Shimbun* that I was able to get an insight into the lives of hundreds of Japanese men and women of all ages, and begin to understand what the Japanese are like today.

I first noticed that such column was being published at the beginning of April 1989, when the "consumption tax" was imposed, according to my wife, with the object of diminishing the "financial deficit" of the ruling political party, and repair the damage done to its reputation by the revelations about the Recruit affair.

I found the letters so interesting that I requested the editor to send me a copy of all those that had appeared until then.

They were much more enlightening than any book about Japan and the Japanese.

After reading the contributions in which common people were writing about their economical situation, the education they had received about money matters, their way of life, their reflections on the dramatic changes brought about by the policy of the government, the affluence of a small sector of the population and the meager budget of most working people, the inadequacies of social welfare and the oppressive taxation, I had the impression that for the first time I had come into contact with the real Japan.

But of course, it was just an impression—and the impression of a bewildered man who had been thrown out of his Japanese ivory tower after living in it for more than 14 years.

5

"OH, NO! NO! WHAT? WELL . . . I . . . I DIDN'T KNOW."

It would be an exaggeration to affirm that all Japanese policitians are despicable individuals without any sense of ethics or morality. I am sure that among them, there are many respectable people with an ideal, who are really trying to do their best for the welfare of the people and the prosperity of the country.

But it is an undeniable fact that some leading politicians go to such an extreme of corruption and immorality that when you read the headlines of the newspapers, you wonder whether it is all a bad dream.

I have never taken an active interest in politics, and I am not going to write at length on the subject.

I do not know whether such a scandal as the

Recruit affair might occur in Europe or in America. But even if it did, the way Japanese politicians implicated in it justified themselves is unthinkable in any other country in the world.

If only one of them had said that he did not know that he had received an astronomical sum as "political contribution," because his secretary had accepted it without telling him anything about it, he might have been believed by somebody. But all of them said the same thing, and used almost the same words.

"No! No! What? Well . . . I'm sorry. I didn't know. You see, my secretary . . . It was my secretary."

"What? Well . . . I'm sorry. I didn't know. You see, my secretary . . . It was my secretary."

"I'm sorry. I didn't know. You see . . . It was my wife."

"What? I . . . I'm sorry. It was . . . Who was it? I will ask my secretary again."

And is it possible to imagine that there may be a prime minister in a Western country, who after admitting that his secretary and his wife had received hundreds of millions of yen "without his knowledge," would speak about political reform, and insist that he would not resign until he accomplished his noble goal of purifying the party?

On April 17, 1989, a journalist who had been sent to Europe on the day it was revealed that former Primer Minister Noboru Takeshita had received an enormous amount of money from Recruit, wrote in the *Asahi Shimbun* about his experience in Paris.

The news that Recruit had paid the equivalent of one million francs in order to attend Takeshita's party, was published in all French newspapers and broadcast by radio and television.

"Oh, are you a Japanese journalist? I have just heard the news . . . Your prime minister . . ."

"One million francs for a ticket!"

When he came back to Japan, the amount that Takeshita admitted he had received from Recruit had already increased to the equivalent of more than seven million francs.

And the amount that had been found in a bamboo thicket had increased to more than ¥200,000,000!

An American friend of mine teased me when I told him how astonished I was at the news that ¥200,000,000 had been found in a bamboo thicket.

"I'm not surprised at all. I have been in this country of economic animals long enough to know them very well. Instead of wasting your time analyzing the syntactic structure of the Japanese language, hadn't you better begin a thorough analysis of the botanical structure and the contents of Japanese bushes?"

I retorted that in a "country of economic animals," the fact that the people—in most cases garbage collectors—who find bundles of ¥10,000 bills invariably hand them over to the police, is astonishing, too.

"If you know the Japanese so well, you must be able to explain to me why common people who are not exactly rich let go such a good chance of lining their pockets."

He scratched his head, and did not know what to say.

6

EVEN LIARS SOMETIMES MAY BE TELLING THE TRUTH

If I had met the American columnist when Takeshita became the new leader of Japan, and had expressed the opinion that there might be some truth in what politicians were saying about their lack of knowledge of the contributions they had received from Recruit, he would not have thought that I was an old fool living in an ivory tower, but an old hand living off the fat of the land, thanks to my connections with them.

Still, the possibility that not all of them were lying cannot be excluded.

The close connection between politics and business, which is typically Japanese, is so peculiar, and the way political contributions are manipulated in order to find loopholes in the law is so complicated, that it is not unlikely that only secretaries, or former secretaries, who handle billions of yen, know how many millions have been received on a certain occasion, by whom and for what reason or purpose they have been received, in whose name and in which account they have been deposited.

On the other hand, although everybody speaks about the "corruption" of politicians, when you are told about the enormous amounts of money that they have to spend for their political activity and their success within the intricate party system, you wonder to what extent it is corruption in the Western meaning of the word.

For instance, a 61-year-old executive who wrote a letter to the editor of *Okane*, dated March 17, 1989, after reading an editorial of the *Asahi Shimbun* which suggested that contributions to electoral districts should be abolished completely, told his own experience about such custom.

Recently, he had gone back to his hometown in Yamanashi, in order to attend the funeral of one of his relatives, a farmer who had no connections with politics or politicians.

He was extremely surprised to see a huge wreath sent by a well-known politician. As it was highly improbable that the dead relative had ever met such a politician, he asked a member of the family about it.

He was told that nobody had contacted him or informed him about the funeral, but as in each electoral district there was a representative of the Liberal-Democratic Party, flowers, saké and all sorts of presents were automatically sent to the house of families that were celebrating a wedding or holding a funeral. And the wreaths were so cumbersome that they often constituted a real nuisance, because they had not enough space, and did not know where to put them.

The writer of this letter was convinced that the root of all evils in the political world lies in the way politicians spend huge amounts of money and the unscrupulous way in which they obtain it. He concluded by saying : "The people are not stupid."

That was not the opinion of an American resident who, in a letter to the editor of *The Japan Times*, dated April 12, 1989, said that the way the "tax reform bill" was railroaded through the Diet made him believe that the people here are indeed fools. As an American the main thing he was confused about was why the people of Japan were allowing it to happen at all.

According to him, taxing the poor is not the best way, and with this tax problem and the ever-growing Recruit scandal, the current leaders responsible, especially the prime minister, were only interested in their own personal gain.

His conclusion was that unless the leadership that is now in power is changed, "all who live here are April Fools."

But the generalization about "all who live here" would be possible only if the Japanese people had the same psychological structure as ours, which is not the case.

For instance, if the same scandal and the same imposition of the same strange tax had taken place in a European country, and the people of that country had let it happen in the same way as the Japanese did, which of course is unthinkable, an American residing there would surely have said that everybody had suddenly become stupid, and he would have been right.

But Japan is neither Europe nor America, and what is foolishness in Europe or America is not necessarily foolishness in Japan.

Although as a European I could not help feeling astonished at the passivity and apathy on the part of the people, I felt sure that they were sick and tired of the arrogance of a lot of politicians of the ruling party, and sooner or later would put a stop to their omnipotence.

None of my Western friends agreed with me. One of them said:

"The only thing you know about Japan is its language. Six months from now, the Japanese will have forgotten all about Recruit and geishas, and will be paying a 9.99% consumption tax."

Another one asked me if I knew the meaning of a common daily expression, *shikata ga nai* (there's nothing we can do about it).

7

APRIL FOOLS ARE NOT NECESSARILY FOOLS

On April 10, 1989, two days before the letter of the foreign resident who said that all of us in this country are April fools was published in *The Japan Times*, a 27-year-old Japanese employee wrote a letter to the readers'column *Koe* (Voice) of the *Asahi Shimbun*, in which he said that, in spite of the violent opposition which was being voiced against the consumption tax, he was basically in favor of it, although he admitted that it needed some revisions.

In his opinion, the object of the new tax was the elimination of the financial deficit of the nation, which has reached a critical point. With his salary, he would not be better off after paying it, but the deficit will not disappear without some sacrifice on the part of the people, and the only way out is a tax increase.

To those who were saying : "Don't torture the

people," he would like to ask how on earth they thought it would be possible to improve the financial situation of the country. And if anybody told him : "That is not my business," he would not tolerate it.

In his opinion, the consumption tax was introduced for the welfare of the nation, and the people, who are enjoying all the benefits of social welfare, should not turn a deaf ear when the government asks for their cooperation.

If the American resident in question had read this letter, he would have reached the conclusion that there were Japanese who are more foolish than he had thought, and that "April fools" was not a mere figure of speech.

To be honest, after reading hundreds of letters to the editor against the consumption tax, I was astonished when I came across this one, and I had a vague feeling that probably it had been written by some leading politician's secretary. Of course, it was a ridiculous doubt.

I felt somewhat suspicious, because I had read that a journal published by the Labor Ministry, in which all Japanese newspapers were harshly criticized as reporting a "bunch of lies" about the Recruit affair, was hastily withdrawn from circulation, after it came to light that also the Labor Ministry was involved in the scandal.

What sounded incredible in this young man's letter, was his reference to social welfare, and his indignation at people who turn a deaf ear while enjoying all the benefits of it.

Unless the letters published in the *Asahi Shimbun* also contain a "bunch of lies," as the writer of the article in the journal of the Labor Ministry said about the reporting of the Recruit affair, it is very hard to imagine that the coffers of the nation are almost empty owing to the fact that too much money is spent on social welfare.

As a matter of fact, the "benefits of social welfare" that Japanese workers are receiving now that Japan has become an economic super-power, in some cases are scantier than those received by Italian workmen half a century ago, when Italy was a very poor country ruled by Fascism.

For instance, in a letter to the editor of *Okane*, dated November 5, 1988, a 63-year-old man said that after working for a period of 10 years in a factory, going in and out of a refrigerator, his left arm froze, and as a consequence of it, he could not go on working.

His doctor was very pessimistic about his recovery, and he was obliged to leave the company. He was 57 years old, and being unable to work in order to earn his living, decided that the only option he had was to commit suicide. But when he went to the place he had chosen for his suicide, a seven-story building, and looked up, he had not the courage to do so.

I simply could not believe my own eyes when I was reading this letter, and remembered what happened to my father when I was a boy.

My father was an artisan. One day, when he was working in the cathedral of my hometown, he fell from a ladder, and broke his leg. He was unable to work for more than a year. He got, of course, free medical treatment and living expenses, and an amount of money that allowed him to buy a large house in the suburbs of our hometown.

To give another example, a friend of my father's, who was in the employ of a small factory in Rome, had an accident while working, and his right arm was amputated. He was about 40 at the time. Of course, he got compensation and a pension.

It is not clear from the letter of this contributor why he did not get a similar treatment, and I cannot jump to a conclusion without knowing all the circumstances of the case.

However, the case of a man who, after working for ten years in a factory and became physically disabled as a consequence of the kind of work he was doing, finds himself in such a plight that the only thing he can do is commit suicide, sounds like something that in Europe might have only been possible more than a century ago.

But a Japanese friend of mine told me that if I go on reading Japanese newspapers, I will find articles about Japanese workmen that will remind me of what I have read in history books about the social welfare enjoyed by the work-men who built the Pyramid of Cheops.

8

SOCIAL WELFARE IN JAPAN

As far as social welfare is concerned, I am not in a position to compare Japan with Italy or any other Western country, for the simple reason that in the last 10 years I have never travelled overseas.

However, after reading the letter which a 62-year-old Japanese pensioner contributed to *Okane* on November 9, 1988, I do not think that Europeans who live on a pension are in the same plight as their Japanese counterparts—but of course, I may be wrong.

This pensioner, who retired at 60, has a heart condition which makes it impossible for him to go on working, and his wife is suffering from rheumatism.

As the pension he is getting is a mere pittance, he used all his savings to buy an old house in the middle of a mountain, where winter is tremendously cold. He did so because he thought he could live cheaply.

But it was a mere illusion. After paying all the taxes and the medical expenses, which even in the case of pensioners are exorbitant, and the bills for electricity, telephone and so on, half of his monthly allowance is gone.

Even if he were in good health, and able to work, it would be impossible to find a job in the middle of the mountain.

As the days go by, it is getting colder, and it will not be long before there will be a heavy snowfall. He would like to buy his poor wife a stove that he saw in an advertisement, but when he thinks of the future, he dare not incur such an expense.

At night he can hardly get a wink of sleep worrying about the future, and what is awaiting both of them. When he watches television, and sees the tall buildings and the bustling streets of the city, he has a feeling of emptiness, as if it were all a dream.

Old age is miserable without money, and he tries to find consolation listening to the chirping of the unknown birds that surround them.

Are the coffers of the nation almost empty because of this kind of social welfare?

The young man who wrote a letter supporting the introduction of the consumption tax said that he would not be better off after paying it. But probably he did not know whether he would suffer as much as old people who go on living thanks to the generosity of such social welfare.

One can get an idea of how elderly people, who have not been able to accumulate enormous amounts of money like the politicians who imposed it, will find difficulty in paying it, by reading the letter to the editor of *Okane* dated March 25, 1989, by a 59-year-old pensioner who up to now has been able to manage financially on savings and retirement pay.

Last year the *maruyū* (tax-exempt small-sum savings system) was abolished. With the new 3% tax, life would become more difficult—and the heartless indifference of the Liberal-Democratic Party towards the people at the bottom of the social ladder more evident.

In the case of this pensioner, the consumption tax means an extra ¥6,000 a month.

What is ¥6,000 nowadays? A trifling sum. The question is how to earn it.

¥6,000 is a lot of money for people like this contributor. But of course it is not for the Minister of Finance, who said, as if it were the most natural thing to say, that not all the money that would be collected as consumption tax would be for the coffers of the nation : the amount that would be pocketed by the businessmen who had collected it would be about ¥500 billion.

By the way, the collection of this tax is very simple : whenever you have to pay for anything you buy or any service you get anywhere, an extra 3% will be added to your bill.

In Japanese it is called *shōhizei*, and the leaders of the ruling party who imposed it, dogmatically asserted that the same tax exists in Europe and America.

I do not think there are many European or American residents in Japan who will agree that it is exactly the same, although it is similar—and some of them will probably say that it is as similar to what in Europe and America is called consumption or sales tax as *udon* is similar to spaghetti, or *sushi* to pizza. For *shōhizei* covers a long list of items that are not taxed in any other industrialized country in the world, such as rent, public utility services, train fares, medicines, a woman's pregnancy (!), postage stamps, etc., etc.

But the the politicians who railroaded the "tax reform bill" through the Diet insist that it is not so bad as many people think. If you ask them why, they will tell you that, for example, they have reduced taxes on luxury items!

Of course, if you are one of those who buy a new Mercedes-Benz or Rolls-Royce every year, have beautiful mink coats or enormous diamond rings especially made for their wives, their girl friends or their geishas, you will be happy and thankful for this fantastic tax reform, which will allow you to lay aside a few more billion yen in order to provide for a rainy day.

The destination of *shōhizei* is an impenetrable mystery, because there are a lot of strange exceptions and complicated clauses which nobody understands.

To give an example of how mysterious it is, suffice it to say that in the case of a businessman with an annual income of ¥30,000,000 or less, he will collect it and pocket it, as he is exempted from handing it over to the Tax Bureau.

Why? Nobody knows, except the politicians who have imposed this tax and the businessmen who benefit from it.

Nobody knows, either, how many businessmen will report an income of more than ¥30,000,000.

For instance, at the beginning of July, 1989, the former managing director of the *Seikyo Shimbun* admitted that he was the owner of a safe containing ¥170,000,000 in cash which had been found at a Yokohama garbage disposal site a few days before.

He said that he had somehow managed to earn such an amount of money about 20 years ago, and was so absent-minded that he had not only forgotten to report it to the tax office, but also the very existence of the money and the safe into which he had put it!

The other day I met again the American who told me that he was not surprised when ¥200,000,000 had been found in a bamboo thicket, and advised me to analyze the botanical structure of Japanese bushes instead of the syntactic structure of the Japanese language.

This time he said :

"The next news will be that a Japanese businessman who has just bought one fourth of the United States and two thirds of all the shares on the Tokyo Stock Exchange has never in his life reported any income at all."

And then he added :

"By the way, last night I dreamed that you and I had got a part-time job at a garbage disposal site full of old safes and surrounded by bushes."

9

THE MOST EXPENSIVE
LAND IN OUR GALAXY

When I told a European tourist that the rent of a small apartment in the Tokyo area is higher than a suite in an expensive hotel in a Western country, he said that he already knew that.

And when I went on to say that in order to rent it, you have to pay a deposit, which is generally the equivalent of two or three months' rent, and what is called *reikin* (generally translated as "key money"), which is also the equivalent of two or three months' rent, he pointed out that neither the deposit nor the key money were peculiar to Japan.

"Of course. But what is peculiar to Japan is the fact that the *reikin* must be paid each time you renew the contract, that is to say, every two years. And the increase of the rent, and the *reikin*, bears no relation to the increase of your salary."

"Is that really so? It's simply incredible."

But there were other incredible things that he did not know.

"Now that the consumption tax has been imposed on anything that you get by paying money, 3% will be added to the deposit, the rent and the *reikin*."

"Is that all?"

"No, it isn't. After paying the deposit, the *reikin*, the rent and the commission to the real estate company, in order to reside in it, you will have to pay a residence tax."

"A what?"

"A residence tax. And it must be paid by you, your wife, your children and your grand-children, if they work and live with you."

As a 54-year-old Japanese housewife says in a letter to *Okane*, dated April 28, 1989, that in this country you must pay "taxes which can only be described as cruel on everything, with the only exception of the air you breathe."

I should like to remind this lady that there is another exception: you are not yet required to pay a consumption tax on taxes, although the payment of taxes is a "consumption," too.

However, the residence tax, which amounts to a sum of money not much smaller that your income tax, can also only be described as "cruel." The only difference between the Deposit-plus-*Reikin*-plus-Rent-plus-Commission-plus-Consumption Tax and the Residence Tax, lies in the fact that in return for the former you get a place to live in, while in the the case of the latter, as a Japanese was telling me the other day, only God and the Tax Bureau know what you get in return for it.

When he told me that, I remembered a big advertisement which was hanging from the roof of the train, and I thought that the reason why only God and the Tax Bureau know the final destination of taxes is not because the Government neglects propaganda or fails to enlighten the public.

The real reason for such gross ignorance on the part of the people is the fact that the method used by the Government in order to make this kind of propaganda arouses more doubts than it dispels.

The advertisement I saw was about a tax which is called *tozei*, which according to Kenkyusha's *New Japanese-English Dictionary* means: "the metropolitan tax; the *To* tax."

As taxes are automatically deducted from my monthly salary, when I go to the tax office for the *kakutei shinkoku* (final income tax return for the year) with the *gensen chōshū* (taxation at the source of income) documents, I ask the employee in charge of the Foreigners' Section to make the necessary calculations for me, and just sign where he tells me to. All I know about the taxation system of Japan is that the list of taxes which are collected directly or indirectly, with or without your knowledge, somehow and somewhere, is too long and too complicated for a layman like me. Therefore, I do not know whether *tozei* is only a synonym of *jūminzei* (residence tax) or just another one among them. In any case, it must be a typically Japanese tax, for otherwise the compilers of the dictionary would not have felt the need of adding the hybrid translation "*To* tax."

The illustration of the advertisement, in full colour, was a real work of art. It was the picture of several beautiful flowers of different sizes, and under each one of them there was a legend and a sum of money that at first I thought were the name of the flower and its price.

But when I began to read, I realized that it was not the ad of a first-class floriculturist, but the propaganda of the Tax Bureau, explaining on what each ¥10,000 collected as "*To* tax" is spent. The legend under each flowers was: "Such and such a sum is spent on such and such an item in order that the people may enjoy such and such a benefit."

I only remember that under the smallest flower there was the legend "¥250 is for the Health of the People," and under the last flower, which was one of the biggest, there was the legend "et cetera."

Good Heavens! On what is this "et cetera" spent? Don't the Japanese people who see this propaganda expect a little more detailed explanation of it?

If there was not enough space, why not eliminate such a trifling item as "¥250 for the Health of the People?"

By the way, since I began to read the readers' column of the *Asahi Shimbun*, the topic of my conversations with my Japanese friends and acquaintances changed from Japanese syntax to money, politics and taxes.

When I told one of them about the flowers of the Tax Bureau, he laughed, and asked me if I had seen the propaganda for the consumption tax.

"Not yet. But judging from the way it was advertised by Takeshita, who in the presence of journalists and cameramen went to an exclusive shop, bought a tremendously expensive necktie, and paid with a beaming face the 3% tax, I do not think it must be very convincing. Unless you have as much money as he has, and buy the same kind of neckties as he does."

"Or unless you dislike a prime minister without a refined taste who spends his money, or yours, on cheap and ugly things in third-class supermarkets."

10

THE HOUSE IS YOURS
BUT. . .

When I was living in my ivory tower, I believed that the great majority of Japanese about my age, like all my colleagues, have a house of their own. And as they do not have to pay rent and so forth, they could not care less about the incredible increase of land prices in Japan, which for some mysterious reason appear to have been brought about by the ruling party.

But judging from what a number of Japanese say in their contributions to *Okane*, I was wrong about this, too.

For example, a 65-year-old Japanese man, in a letter dated October 26, 1988, said that when he received from the landowner a letter written with a word processor, he felt the same tension as he did when he received the draft card. After a series of periodical increases in the last few years, the owner was demanding one more.

This contributor is one of those Japanese who have built their house on leased land.

His income is always the same, living expenses are higher than ever, and the implacable increase of land, which goes on without any limits, is becoming a nightmare. And he fears that it will not be long before he will have to pay more to live in "his" house than in a rented one.

Therefore, he is full of anxiety about the future.

As far as I know, neither in Europe nor in America is there such a custom as building one's own house on leased land. In Japanese it is called *shakuchi*, and I must have read or heard about it since I came to Japan. But until I read this letter, I had forgotten it completely.

In any case, on account of the increase in the lease of the land, there are also Japanese people who have had to abandon the house in which their families had been living for generations.

A 74-year-old housewife, in a letter dated September 27, 1988, told her own painful experience. On account of the increases which she had to pay year after year, at last she could not afford to go on living in the house that she had inherited from her father and mother in law, and had to return the land to the owner.

With tears in her eyes, she separated from all her friends and acquaintances, and went away from the house where she had been living for many long years.

She said that the first and second-generation owners of the land were people "with feelings," but the third-generation owner was "modern," and told her that if she agreed to pay without a receipt, he would reduce the amount of the increase a little. She was foolish enough to do so, thinking that in her economical situation any discount she could get would help.

And when she realized that it was absolutely necessary to get a receipt, hated herself for having being so ingenuous and immature as to accept the proposition of such an unscrupulous owner.

I have no comments to make.

11

HOW TO LIVE RENT-FREE IN JAPAN

I do not think that nowadays there are people who are so reckless as to build their house on leased land, and it is quite probable that the custom of *shakuchi* is dying out.

Therefore, you may safely assume that in future nobody will be evicted from his own house because of lack of money to pay the "rent" of the land where they built it.

But there are millions of Japanese employees who will be evicted from the houses and apartments that do not belong to them, and in which they are living without paying any rent at all, or only a very small monthly sum of money.

These houses or apartments are called *shataku*, which means "company house or apartment," and they are not necessarily "rabbit hutches," at least in the case of executives. They either belong to the company or are rented by it for its employees.

Another version of *shataku* are the so-called *kōsha*, or apartments belonging to the Government, in order to accomodate public servants.

Employees and public servants can lead a happy and care-free life in these *shataku* or *kōsha* until they retire, without having to worry about such matters as the increase of land prices. And in the opinion of a Japanese acquaintance of my wife's, some of them probably do not care too much about how many million yen politicians have to spend on geishas in order to find some kind of solace after a hard day's work and the tension they accumulate trying to figure out how to impose new taxes for the Welfare of the People.

But when employees and public servants retire, according to a Japanese pessimistic fellow who was speaking the other day about his vision of the future of young people, they will get from the company or the Government a lump retirement grant which will not be even enough to buy a square inch of land in Tokyo, and/or a pension that will be enough to pay the taxes on the pension, two *sushi* a day and the consumption tax on one of them.

Of course, you cannot rely on pessimists to get

an objective image of the situation as it is now, and the way things will turn out in the remote future.

Therefore, I will tell you what a 57-year-old public servant, in a letter to the editor of *Okane*, dated September 2, 1988, is writing about a friend of his who will retire next year.

His friend, who is also a public servant, has spent 40 years of his life being transferred from one place to the other. Owing to the enormous educational expenses of his three sons, and the money he has had to pay for their living expenses in Tokyo, where they attended a private university, he was unable to buy a house even at the time when land prices were not so high as they are now.

But next year, he will have to leave the *kōsha*, which belongs to the Government. He will get ¥20,000,000, with which he will not be able to buy even a rabbit hutch.

The writer of this letter is reflecting with bitterness that working 40 years, and being thrown out on the streets is the destiny of common people in Japan. And while politicians collect hundreds of millions of yen in one single fund-raising party, and one of them boasted in the Diet that he was wearing a suit which costs ¥200,000, and a necktie that costs ¥20,000, a poor public servant who has been working all his life has not even enough money to buy a strip of land as large as a"cat's forehead."

By the way, my wife told me the other day that she has read an article in *The Japan Times* about a Japanese journalist who travelled to Italy, and decided to buy an Italian necktie that in Japan costs ¥20,000, hoping that in Italy it would cost much less. He went from shop to shop all over the city (she does not remember whether it was Milan or another city), but could not find it anywhere, and nobody knew about it — not even the manufacturer's agent. "Why don't you buy it in Japan?" they asked him. Such neckties are probably made exclusively for export to the Land of Money, where only people like the politician mentioned by this contributor earn enough to buy them.

Another contributor, a 45-years-old housewife, in a letter dated October 4, 1988, said that until recently she had never thought of a home of her own, because her husband has been transferred by the company from city to city, and in each one of them the company has a comfortable *shataku* in a first-class residential district.

But her husband is now 55, and five years

from now they will be thrown out of the *shataku*. And she is beginning to worry about the future, and for the first time she is realizing that in this country, you work all your life for the company, and when you retire you have not even an apartment or a house of your own.

Her husband, who has not the least idea of the family budget, relies on their savings in order to buy a place to live in "wherever it is possible."

From now on they will try to save as much money as they can, and she warned her son, who last year entered the university, to study hard in order to graduate in four years.

She said that in her indignation, when she realized the situation, she exclaimed : "It's the politicians' fault!"

I do not think that anybody can blame her for saying that. Except the politicians who are living in a small and uncomfortable *shataku* or *kōsha*, and will be given a pension smaller than the one her husband will get—if such politicians exist in this country.

12

THE TIME CAPSULE TIME DEPOSIT IN THE BANK OF HAPPINESS

Although Japan is not exactly the kind of country where the average working man can look forward to a bright future, owing to the absurd price of land, sky-high rent, meager pension and inadequate social welfare, there are banks that promise a bright future in exchange for a small deposit.

According to an article by Bob Horiguchi, which was published in *The Japan Times* on June 28, 1989, there are people who, thanks to a golden opportunity offered by the Shiawase Bank, which means "The Bank of Happiness," in Yamagata Prefecture, are investing ¥50,000, which is guaranteed to grow to ¥900,000,000 or even ¥9,900,000,000 in future!!!

The only snag is that the future of this

wonderful Get-Rich Plan, which is named the
Shiawase Time Capsule Time Deposit, is a little
too remote. For only in 250 years' time will the
proceeds from the initial deposit reach the
predicted sums.

A lot of customers of this generous bank have
already signed on to this marvelous scheme. And
they are well aware that it is not they, but their
distant descendants who will (?) benefit from it.

Isn't that optimism and faith in the future?
And who can say that the people of Japan are
living in the present after hearing that no less
than 20,000 Japanese have already deposited
¥50,000 in this wonderful bank?

But I have bad luck, and whenever I get into a
casual conversation with Japanese young men,
they tell me that they do not care about the
future. And if they are old, they are all
pessimistic not only about the future, but also
about the present.

One of the latter yesterday told me that the
social system which has been created by the
ruling Liberal-Democratic Party is as liberal
and as democratic as it was in the feudal age.
The only difference is that feudal lords are no
longer called feudal lords, the vassals who work
like slaves for them call themselves "middle-
class people," and the chains with which they

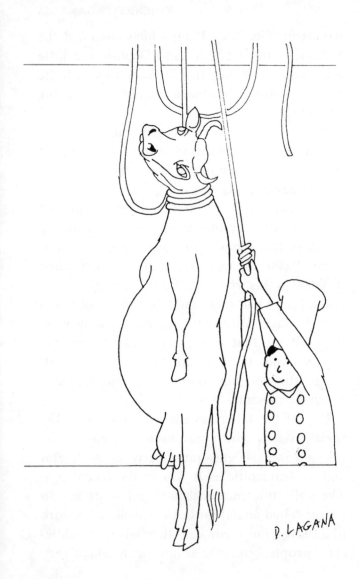

D. LAGANA

are tied unto them are not of iron, but of an invisible synthetic fiber much stronger than steel.

When he told me that, I laughed. But he did not. On the contrary, he looked at me with anger in his eyes.

It was the first time in my life that I met a fellow who says humorous things, and has no sense of humor.

I console myself by thinking that one of these days my luck will change, and that the fellow sitting next to me at the snack bar will be one of the executives of the Bank of Happiness. But the consolation lasts only an instant. For the executives of this Bank, if they do sometimes come to Tokyo to look for new customers, will probably go to a restaurant which was recently inaugurated in Shinjuku, and where they charge you ¥100,000 for a steak.

It is not a steak of solid gold, or wrapped in a gold plate, as the *sushi* I was told about by a friend of mine. It is a cut from a champion breed of beef the name of which I have forgotten.

The bottle of wine they will uncork for the Super-Gourmets who eat the Super-Steak will be the Super-Wine—and for the latter they will charge the same price as an eatery I am going to write about later.

According to *Shukan Yomiuri,* the owner

of the restaurant revealed to the journalist who interviewed him that his patronage comes from "religious and educational connections."

As a man engaged in educational activities, I make a solemn statement under oath that I have never crossed the threshold of this eating house. And I also swear to God and Buddha that I am not so forgetful as the owner of the safe found at the garbage disposal site, who was engaged in religious activities.

13

HOW TO CRACK A JOKE
IN JAPAN

It is often said that the Japanese people have no sense of humor. This is a generalization made by foreigners who have too much of it, and accepted as gospel truth by those Japanese who happen to lack it.

I knew about this generalization before I came to Japan.

If I can trust my memory, I read about it for the first time when I was learning the Japanese language by myself with the help of a big Japanese-English dictionary. It was compiled by a famous Japanese lexicographer, who in order to explain the different shades of meaning of the Japanese verb *kaisuru*, which corresponds to the English verbs "interpret," "comprehend," etc. gave as an example the expression "The Japanese people do not understand humor."

When I came across this example, I was rolling with laughter over a novel by Soseki Natsume, which I enjoyed more than Dickens' *Pickwick Papers*.

You can easily imagine up to what extent I believed what the lexicographer in question was saying about his fellow countrymen. And I was not too far from the truth when I drew the conclusion that the Japanologists who first contributed to the diffusion of this generalization had probably had the misfortune of only coming into contact with people like him. And they did not, or could not, reflect that people like him were to be found in their own country, too.

But birds of one feather flock together, and it is also possible that those Japanologists only mixed with Japanese people towards whom they felt an ineffable spiritual affinity.

However, I always thought that, generally speaking, the Japanese people have as much sense of humor as Western people, or at least as much as Germans, who are also said to be rather slow in understanding the point of a joke.

Consequently, when I obtained a fellowship from the Japan Foundation, and began to write a weekly column in the *Asahi Shimbun*, I did not hesitate in filling it with jokes and ironical remarks about the Japanese and their way of life.

I am a modest man. But not too modest. And I am not going to say that my column was not popular, and deny the fact that thanks to it I became famous all over Japan.

I received hundreds of letters from my readers, and although some of them did contradict what I said, also in a humorous way, and in the same way I answered in my column, I was under the impression that none of them had felt insulted or hurt.

But judging from the reaction of a man with a Japanese name who wrote a letter to the editor of the *Asahi Evening News* about my column, there were also readers who did.

It was my wife who showed it to me a few days before we left Japan. It was very long, and I do not remember exactly what was written in it. What attracted my attention was a paragraph in which he said that the Japanese understand and enjoy a joke about them when a foreigner makes it in English, but when he does it in perfect Japanese, they simply hate it, even if it is exactly the same joke.

He said that I can write in Japanese better than the average Japanese and ought to know the meaning of the Japanese verb *aratamaru*, which is difficult to translate into English (it means : become formal, use formal language, stand on ceremony, be ceremonious, serious, etc.), and moderate my humorous tone.

I had never written in English either in that newspaper or in any other, and I could never understand why the writer of that letter thought it fit to give a sermon about me in English and to foreign residents who did not know me.

If that letter had been written in Japanese and had been the only one I had received personally from a Japanese reader of my column, I would have remembered what the lexicographer affirmed about the Japanese, and followed the reader's advice. Or I would have stopped writing in Japanese and begun to write in English for foreign residents—and for the Japanese who only enjoy jokes about them in English.

In my opinion, if you are, for instance, an Englishman and you crack a joke or make a humorous remark about the fellow countrymen of the person with whom you are talking, unpleasant misunderstandings are likely to arise, in the first place, when you do it in English and he or she has a poor knowledge of it, or when you do in his or her language and you do not master it.

If the writer of the letter had said that I had better stop joking in broken Japanese, I might have agreed. But he said that my Japanese was perfect. If so, why lay such emphasis on the language?

On the other hand, mere mastery of the language does not guarantee perfect comprehension of humor. For humor differs not only between one nationality and another, but also from one individual to the other, and there are times when you miss the point of a humorous remark made by your best friend.

To give a concrete example, Shigenobu Sakano, Home Affairs Minister of the Cabinet formed by Sousuke Uno, said that the consumption tax should be 4% instead of 3%, because 4 was an even number. . . It was a joke! (By the way, in Japanese, 4 is pronounced *shi*, which also means "death," and is a number which is considered as lucky as 13 is in the West.)

Nobody understood it. And the people who listened to him were so angry, that he had to explain that he was just joking when he made the remark, and apologize deeply.

And Hisao Horinouchi, Minister of Agriculture, Forestry and Fisheries, in a campaign speech for the Upper House election which took place on July 23, 1989, said that "women are useless in the world of politics," referring to the recent victories of women in local elections. . .

Surprised at the sensation his words caused, he had to retract all the remarks the next day.

"My real intention was not correctly reported. I humbly apologize for any inconvenience I have caused," he said.

He did not explain what his real intention was. Perhaps he was joking, too — or it was just a slip of the tongue.

A few days after apologizing for the remark about the uselessness of women in politics, he put his foot in his mouth again, during another campaign tour.

This time he told a gathering of farmers, who are traditional supporters of the Liberal-Democratic Party, that they can *nekobaba* (which means "embezzle" or "pocket," and is not exactly a very refined Japanese expression) only half the profits which an exemption measure in the consumption tax brings to farmers with an annual income of ¥30,000,000 or less!

But probably this was neither a joke nor a lapsus linguae. For shortly after the Upper House elections, in which the ruling party suffered a horrible defeat, Construction Minister Takeshi Noda claimed that farmers are not paying their income taxes and said they are ignoring the fact that the introduction of the income tax was accompanied by income tax reductions.

"When we talk about the income tax cuts in farming villages, the farmers turn a deaf ear. This is because there are no farmers paying income taxes."

And according to *Newsweek*, dated July 31, 1989, Nagasaki Congressman Kuro Matsuda said about Japan's farmers who would lose their jobs if food imports rose :

"They will only be able to work with their bodies, because they don't have any brains."

Newsweek does not specificy whether he said that before or after what Max Lerner, an American columnist, defined as the "Humpty-Dumpty electoral fall."

14

THE PLEASANT ATMOSPHERE OF THE TAX OFFICE

As I have already said, I flatter myself that I have mastered the Japanese language, and know its subtle shades of meaning. Still, I cannot understand the jokes of some Japanese.

What baffles me most is the delicate and exquisite sense of humor (?) of the artists who conceive the advertisements of the Tax Bureau of Japan, and the people who hang them on the walls of the tax office as if they were masterpieces that will delight the taxpayers who have to go there on March 15 in order to make their contribution to the Wealth of the Nation and the Welfare of the People.

When I went to the tax office last year, there were two large ads in full color hanging on the wall.

One of them was the photograph of a handsome man in his early forties with a beaming face full of pride and expectation, as if he had just received an invitation to a very exclusive banquet to be held in honor of the most powerful politician or the richest businessman in Japan. He was saying: "Me too! Me too! I'm going on March 15, too!"

The second ad, also in full color, was the photograph of a young woman who was so beautiful that she would have won the title of Miss Universe only by sending a picture of her body and the necessary bust and hip meaurements etc. to the organizers of the beauty contest. She was smiling in a coquettish way as if inviting her lover to a secret meeting and saying: "Let's meet at the tax office on March 15!"

The man was really an Adonis. But I am not a woman. The girl was a Venus, and absolutely irresistible. But I am married.

Therefore, I felt as if the officials of the Tax Bureau were adding insult to injury by sadistically making fun of taxpayers.

Of course, I am absolutely sure that neither the Japanese who had made the ads nor the Japanese who had proudly hung them on the wall were sadists. But to describe those ads in a language other than Japanese, there is only one expression: "black humor."

If the Japanese versions of Adonis and Venus had said, with a serious expression on their faces : "It is our duty as good citizens to pay our taxes," or something to that effect, I would not have felt derided. But is there one single individual in the whole Western world who would not see any black humor in those ads?

I approached a Japanese middle-aged man who was waiting for his turn, and asked him:

"Don't you think that those ads are a little funny?"

He looked at them, and said:

"Why do you think they're funny?"

When I explained my impression, he looked at the ads once more, and said, as if speaking to himself :

"Well, the tax office is not exactly a pleasant meeting-place."

And then he added :

"But we don't bother to look at such ads."

A foreigner who had overheard our conversation told me in English with a German accent that probably the officials of the Tax Bureau who had them made had not bothered to look at them either — and that he could not help feeling sorry for the artists of the advertising agencies who had made them.

15

THE ECSTATIC PLEASURE
OF PAYING TAXES

I do not think that there is a country where common people, who earn an annual income that is barely enough to pay food, lodging and the educational expenses of their children, enjoy going to the tax office every year.

I do not think, either, that there is a country in the world where professors who teach in two or three universities, and have to go to the tax office every year in order to pay more taxes in addition to those that have already been automatically deducted from their monthly salary, do not complain at all.

I do not know if the taxes that people like me have to pay in Japan are the most oppressive in the world.

The only thing I do know is that taxes in Japan, in the case of common people, are oppressive. And the only thing I can guarantee is that nobody, except some politicians, all their secretaries, associates, relatives, friends, and some of their geishas, can say that what I am affirming is an exaggeration.

Consequently, few readers will be surprised if I say that I am not in the best of moods when I have to go to the tax office.

But I am a foreigner. What about the Japanese?

Japanese newspapers and magazines are full of articles, commentaries, interviews and letters to the editor about the intolerable burden that a formidable list of taxes constitutes for common people who live on a salary.

I now know that most Japanese do not bother to look at the strange advertisements of the Tax Bureau. And that there are also Japanese taxpayers who feel the same as I do in the atmosphere of the tax office.

As a matter of fact, there is at least one who feels worse than I do when he has to go there.

He is 69 years old. In his letter to the editor of *Okane*, dated December 24, 1989, he said that he has never been able to overcome the terrible shock of the long interrogation he was submitted to when he rebuilt his house.

Although he had nothing to hide and no

intention of evading taxes, he felt as though he were being treated like a suspect when the tax agent interrogated him.

Where had he got the money from? How much money had he got? How had he got it? Was he telling the truth? Where were the documents that proved that he was not lying?

It was such a horrible ordeal, that he could not sleep the whole night, and since then the mere mention of the word "tax office" gives him gooseflesh : he fears tax agents more than policemen.

I remember reading other letters like this one. All of them were written by elderly people or pensioners. But unless my memory is failing me, among these elderly people there was not even one involved, directly or indirectly, with the Recruit affair, or with tax evasion for political reasons.

A Japanese acquaintance of mine told me that also these poor men fighting for an ideal to which they have devoted their entire energies and their whole life, must have been submitted to such a shocking interrogation—and that some of them were probably hospitalized as a consequence of the tremendous stress that followed such treatment.

"Don't you, too, think that each one of them

should be given a gold medal and a cash prize (tax-exempt, of course) of at least one hundred million yen for their dignified silence about such nerve-racking experience?" he said.

16

THE HABITAT OF GOLD-EATING RATIONAL ANIMALS

Of course, there are Japanese people who are looking forward to March 15 with great pleasure. According to a Japanese friend of mine, they are the "Big Bosses"of the Tax Bureau who, out of each ¥10,000 they collect, spend ¥250 for the Health of the People, and a lot more for the mysterious "et cetera."

There must be also Japanese people who will not be exactly happy, but will not care too much even if they have to pay millions and millions more than I do.

And among these patriots, it is possible that there are those Japanese who are regular customers of the restaurant I went to with my wife after leaving the tax office.

The restaurant in question is in the vicinity of Ichigaya Station. From outside it does not look like an expensive one, and my wife suggested that we should go there and enjoy a steak for a change. When we went in, it had all the appearance of a cheap place.

But when the waitress handed me the wine list, and began to read the prices they charged, you could have knocked me down with a feather. In the case of the flowers of the Tax Bureau I only remember the smallest one, but in the case of the bottles of wine of this restaurant, I remember the one with the highest price, i.e. ¥300,000.

No. It is not a printing mistake. In that restaurant they charge you Three Hundred Thousand Yen for a bottle of wine.

Yes. Three Hundred Thousand Yen for a bottle of wine. And believe me, this is not a story I am inventing in order to add a touch of humor to this sad chapter. It is absolutely true.

I looked around, feeling a sinister sensation, took my wife by the hand and ran towards the door, my heart throbbing violently.

Yesterday I told the above-mentioned Japanese friend of mine all about it.

"You are Japanese and surely you must know what kind of people are so rich and have such a strange taste as to pay ¥300,000 for a bottle of wine in that kind of eating house."

"Probably they are the same people who eat gold *sushi*."

"Gold *sushi*? Are you pulling my leg?"

"Of course not. The inside of gold *sushi* is the same as ordinary *sushi*, but instead of seaweed a thin plate of 24-carat gold is used. Gourmets who eat such *sushi* say that gold is good for their health."

"And how much do they charge?"

"I saw a television program about gold *sushi*. I don't remember exactly, but I think it was ten or twenty thousand yen apiece."

It was the first time in my life that I had heard that on this planet there are rational animals that eat 24-carat gold.

17

THE JAPANESE VERSION OF THE HOLY TRINITY REVISED AND CORRECTED

My wife is working as a part-time lecturer, and is earning more than the insignificant amount of money which she is allowed to in order to be considered economically dependent on me.

Consequently, she is excluded from the benefits of what is called *shakai hoken* (social insurance).

As a part-time worker, she can affiliate with what is called *kokumin kenkō hoken* (national health insurance).

What is left of the money she earns as a part-time worker, after paying income tax and residence tax and so forth, which are automatically deducted from her salary every month, is not even enough to pay the rent.

If she decided to affiliate, the benefits she would get would be 70% of her medical expenses, but in practice, for example in the case of hospitalization, each day in hospital would cost her more than a week in a suite of the Waldorf Astoria.

By the way, even in the case of full-time workers, medical care is not completely free, and hospitalization is not exactly cheap, which means that anybody who is working in this country, and has not got a lot of money in the bank, is freed from economic distress.

In order to get a generous 70% of medical expenses, she would have to pay a yearly amount of money which is a little higher than the residence tax, which in turn is, as I have already mentioned, a little lower than income tax.

In a few words, now she is only paying income tax to the *zeimusho* (tax office) and income tax, under a different name, to the *kuyakusho* (ward office). If she affiliated with the *kokumin kenkō hoken*, she would have to pay income tax, for the third time under another name.

Is that all? No, it isn't.

The whole thing is more complicated than some *kanji* characters that are used in family names, and are not not be found in any *kanji* dictionary, including the biggest one, which contains about 50,000 of them. But I will try my best to explain what my wife told me.

If she affiliated with the *kokumin kenkō hoken*, she would be obliged to affiliate also with what is called *kokumin nenkin* (national pension), and would have to pay a fixed amount of money every month. Although this fixed monthly payment is lower than the one she is now paying to the *zeimusho* as income tax, the one that she is paying to the *kuyakusho* as residence tax, and the one she would have to pay to the same *kuyakusho* if she affiliated with the *kokumin kenkō hoken*, in her case, it would be about one third of what she is paying as residence tax, with the only advantage that it would be fixed and would not increase in case she earned more money by working harder as a part-timer.

Unfortunately I am not an expert on the subject, and do not know the exact figures. Therefore, there may be some error, omission, understatement or overstatement in what I am writing about what I believe is the real situation : if so, I humbly apologize in advance to the Tax Bureau authorities and to my readers for any inconvenience the inaccurate information I am giving will cause, and promise to be more careful in future, and devote a couple of months to the study of the taxation system.

However, my wife analyzed the matter with the help of an employee of the *kuyakusho*, and to make things easy for me to understand, she told me that in return for 70% of medical expenses, she would have to pay about four times what in Europe is paid only once as income tax, as if she were not one but four different persons.

To be honest, I did not understand either the explanation or the metaphor.

I asked a Japanese friend to explain things a little more clearly.

"You are a Catholic, aren't you?"

"Yes."

"What is the Holy Trinity?"

"Three Persons, but only one God."

"If your wife affiliated with the People's Health insurance, she would become something like the Holy Quaternity."

"The what?"

"Four Income-Tax Paying Persons, but only One Income-Tax Paying God."

He laughed, and I laughed, too, in order not to disappoint the poor fellow, who was obviously under the illusion that he had cracked the Joke of the Year.

"And the pension she would get," he added, "would be One Third of the Cube Root of One Fourth of the total amount she would pay until the age of Three Score."

18

THE PHILANTHROPIC ACTIVITY OF THE TAX BUREAU OF JAPAN

My wife has little sense of humor, but an acquaintance of hers, who is the wife of a European post-graduate student, has much less. She is a part-time teacher at a tutoring school, and she and her husband have been in Japan for only six months.

When I told my wife what my Japanese friend had said about the "Holy Quaternity," and gave her all the necessary explanations, at last she saw the joke. But when she told it to the post-graduate student's wife, the joke fell on much stronger ground.

She turned pale, and after saying that she had been thinking of affiliating with both the *kokumin kenkō hoken* and the *kokumin nenkin*, began to tremble like a leaf.

She is a devout Catholic, and said that she has no intention of becoming a convert to a strange religious sect where they tell you that if you only contribute most of the money you earn as a part-time worker in order to help your husband, you will have the privilege of becoming the "Holy Quaternity." And that when you become such a mystical Being, the "Great Priests" of the sect will pay part of your medical expenses, if they have the bad luck of your falling a victim to a disease.

"Apostasy is a horrible thing, and you may be sentenced to death if the Great Priest of your religion is somebody like Khomeini. In the case of Catholics, things are different. But apostasy is apostasy."

Besides lacking a sense of humor, the post-graduate student's wife is as stubborn as all women are, except feminists. For feminists have all the virtues and none of the defects of Eve, who according to the Bible was created by God in order to make Adam feel less lonely in the Garden of Eden, with the consequences that everybody knows.

To make a long story short, only a priest could, after six sessions, convince her that it was all a misunderstanding.

The priest explained to her that neither the

kokumin kenkō hoken nor the *kokumin nenkin* are religious sects, but only some sort of typically Japanese philanthropic entities, and affiliating with them might constitute a financial loss or lead to the bankruptcy of the family budget, but it would definitely not be a mortal sin.

And he added that the only purpose of these philanthropic entities appears to be accumulating as much money as possible in order to be able to pay, as I have already mentioned in two or three previous chapters, ¥250 out of each ¥10,000 they collect for the Health of the People.

Thus, the priest put an end to her ordeal—but not to mine.

A few day later, my wife read an article about the most expensive piece of art ever purchased by a municipal government in Japan : the oil painting "Reclining Nude with Hair Undone," by the famous Italian artist Amedeo Modigliani. It was bought by the Osaka city government, and it would be proudly shown off at an exhibition in August 1989.

When she saw the price of the painting— ¥1.93 billion!!!—and its photograph in the newspaper, she said that she could not understand two things : where the money had

D.LAGANA

come from, and why it had been spent on such an "obscene" painting.

About the first question, I ventured the hypothesis that they had bought it with a small percentage of the money which is allotted by the Tax Bureau for the enigmatic "et cetera." She agreed with me.

About the reason why they had bought it, I said that I had no aesthetic objection to it : I explained to her that the painting is definitely not obscene, and that as an Italian I admired the good taste of the Japanese connossoirs who had recommended its purchase. She disagreed. And so did the post-graduate student's wife.

Both of them went to see that priest, showed him the newspaper cutting, and asked him whether I was right or not. He glanced at the photograph, and looked as if he were going to vomit.

And he said something about me that made me wonder whether I had better begin to act like a Japanese *teishu kanpaku* (the opposite of a henpecked husband), and forbid her to see that priest again—and the post-graduate student's wife.

The other day I read in a Japanese newspaper that the city had received letters and telephone calls from a lot of citizens who complained that the painting was not only too expensive, but also too obscene.

By the way, I hope that my readers will be able to distinguish between humorous fiction and harsh reality.

19

ILLNESS IS A FORBIDDEN LUXURY IN JAPAN

Letters to the editor of English-language newspapers are full of complaints about the cost of medical care and the "ridiculous" assistance a part-timer gets in exchange for what a European sarcastically defined as "legalized robbery."

Sarcasm is sarcasm, and the truth is the truth. And the truth is that social welfare in Japan, which is one of the first, if not already the first economic power in the world, can only be compared to social welfare in an underdeveloped country.

As regards medical care, especially in the case of a serious illness that requires hospitalization, the situation with which a part-timer is confronted in this country, is tragic.

If you become the "Holy Quaternity," the "High Priests" will pay 70% of the medical expenses. The snag is not only the sacrifice you will be required to make in order to reach such a privileged status, but also, and especially, the amount of money required to pay the remaining 30%, which in the case of a surgical operation, or a long hospitalization, may be absolutely beyond your means.

In a few words, in this country, if you are young and healthy, or old, healthy and have a chance to go on working like a young man or woman, you may make a decent living even as a part-time worker. But if you fall seriously ill, your situation in this land of money will be pretty much the same as in a backward country.

In Europe, and in any other country with a European social welfare system, there are public hospitals. And public hospital are and will always be public hospitals, where nobody is obliged to pay. And in some cases, no distinction is made between native and foreign citizens, residents and tourists : any human being who goes to a public hospital and needs urgent medical assistance, he or she will get it, and no questions will be asked except his or her name.

I have been told that in some European countries things have changed a lot in the last few years, and there are serious problems of accommodation, long waiting lists and so on. Although also in Japan there are waiting lists, in this sense the situation in some European countries is much worse.

However, in public hospitals that do not charge you one single cent, you cannot expect the same kind of attention and service as in the tremendously expensive hospitals of Japan. But if you can afford to go to a first-class private clinic, you will get it, and for a small fraction of the amount of money that you have to pay in this country.

In Japan there are no public hospitals which are free of charge for anybody under any circumstances and for any reasons whatsoever. Why? Isn't Japan more affluent than any European country?

What is surprising is the fact that not only young and old people who are working, but also those who are living on a pension have to pay enormous amounts of money when they fall ill.

I had an idea of the sad plight into which pensioners find themselves when I read the letter which a 62-year-old widow contributed to *Okane*, dated March 21, 1989.

Her health is failing, and even if she were strong enough to work, nobody would employ a person like her at her age. She is constantly worried about the future, and what will happen to her if she falls ill.

She is receiving a pension which is barely enough to live from hand to mouth. She has laid aside some money, but when she thinks that it would "melt away like light snow" in the case of illness, she hesitates before buying not only a sweater but also underwear, although she would like to look neat and tidy.

Her daughter-in-law told her to try and save as much as possible.

"You know, one month in hospital would cost three hundred thousand yen!" she said.

She is following her advice, but when she could not go on using the same glasses because of the pain in her eyes, and had a new pair made, she went into the red. But if she went on a diet of bread and milk to cover the deficit, she would ruin her health.

She said that she would like to ask the politicians involved in the Recruit scandal on what they spend hundreds and hundreds of million yen.

If you are a foreign part-time worker, you are not affiliated with *kokumin* etc., etc., you have no family, no friends, and need a surgical operation or a long hospitalization beyond your means, what will you do?

I have not the least idea. For detailed information write to the *zeimusho* or *kuyakusho* of any city in Japan.

A few days ago my wife read an article in *The Japan Times* about a young woman who had come to Japan from a South-Asian country and had a part-time job in Tokyo. She fell seriously ill, and as she did not earn enough to pay for medical attention, she did not follow the advice of her friends and acquaintances, and delayed going to hospital until it was too late. She died in hospital, and was posthumously affiliated with the *kokumin* etc., etc. so that the hospital would be able to collect the money that the dead girl ought to have paid.

It was not clear whether the hospital only got from the *kuyakusho* 70% of the total medical expenses, thus sustaining a loss of 30%, and who paid the burial expenses.

If such losses increase, and more oil paintings of Reclining Nudes with Hair Undone are bought for the Enjoyment of the People, I am very much afraid that the flower in the ad of the Tax Bureau which symbolizes the amount spent for the Health of the People will become so

small that you will need a magnifying glass to
appreciate its beauty.

20

"ECONOMIC ANIMALS"
AND
"MONEY- WORSHIPPERS"

Now that Japan has become an economic superpower, there are very few people in the Western world who are not interested in things Japanese, and there is an almost interminable list of books about the Japanese language, history, culture, traditions, way of life, mentality, workaholism, rabbit hutches...and of course, the politicians and the corporations which have transformed Japan into an unassailable citadel of wealth, investment and prosperity.

When I first came here, Japan was not yet a great economic power, and its language and culture only attracted very few foreigners, who were humorously called *hen na gaijin*, which means "strange," or "eccentric foreigners."

There were practically no Japanese-language schools, very few textbooks and dictionaries for foreign students, and no organizations that found part-time jobs for illegal immigrants.

On the other hand, the yen was not so strong as it is now, and not many Japanese people could afford to travel abroad. And there was no "Japan bashing"—or "America bashing."

Life in Japan was much the same as it is now, except for the fact that the cost of living was not so high, and it was relatively easy to find an apartment or a small house for a reasonable rent, although the price of land had already increased, and buying one was beyond my means.

I was fascinated by the country and its people, who were very honest, polite and respectful. And they still are.

In those days, which now seem so remote, you never heard about the extravagant life of luxury of a class of new rich or free spenders on expense accounts of large corporations at home and overseas.

Politicians did not exactly have a good reputation, but you never heard, either, about the corruption and shameless behavior that is becoming notorious all over the world, and giving Japan an extremely ugly image. But the economic power of Japan was increasing rapidly, and the

Japanese people were already being called "economic animals."

Still, the Japanese people I came into contact with were just the opposite of "economic animals." Most of them belonged to the intellectual class, and were generous, disinterested and idealistic people. And in my daily contact with the man in the street, I never met a Japanese who was rude, arrogant, or mercenary—either then or now.

Athough I had read in a couple of novels ironical remarks and humorous episodes about the Osaka merchants who were only thinking about money, and said "Have You Made a Profit Today?" instead of *Konnichi wa* ("Good morning," "Good afternoon," "Hello"), I visited Osaka only once in order to give a lecture, and the people I became acquainted with were not merchants.

But the fact that I never met any materialistic people does not mean that there were none of them.

"Money-worshippers," as they are called by the Japanese who are shocked to see the changes that have taken place in the last few years in the Japanese way of life, have always existed all over the world, and Japan is no exception.

For instance, a Japanese 65-year-old man, in

a contribution to *Okane*, dated September 6, 1988, said that his father was such an extreme "money-worshipper" that he only showed love and affection to those of his children whom he thought capable of making money when they grew up, and treated in an incredibly cold manner those whom he thought incapable of doing so.

This contributor was one of the latter. When he was a secondary school student, in order to get the necessary money for his tuition fees, he had to implore him by bowing with his hands on the table.

As a consequence of such treatment, he began to hate money, and devoted half of his life to things that had nothing to do with money-making. And even now that he is leading a life that might be described as one of luxury, in comparison with the extreme poverty of the past, when there were times he could not even buy an egg, he shivers at the very mention of the word "money."

Although such "money-worshippers" did exist, as the personal experience of this contributor proves beyond doubt, I believe that there were very few of them — at least among the common people.

21

"MONEY - WORSHIPPERS" OR "WORKAHOLICS"?

There are many cases in which you cannot rely on the Japanese-English dictionary in order to know the exact equivalent of a word that is commonly used in everyday conversation.

To give a few examples, according to the dictionary, *seijika* means "politician." But what is political activity here is often what in the West would be called sordid business.

Yūfuku is translated as "affluence" and *kokka* as "nation." But the Japanese equivalent of "affluence of the nation" is the enormous wealth of a few individuals.

The translation of *shūdan* is "group."

The average Japanese employee has to work from morning to night every day of the year except Sundays and a few holidays that can be counted on the fingers on one hand. For what and for whom? For the prosperity of the group.

As a member of that group, will he share its benefits? The answer is "No," unless he happens to be the employer, or one of the leaders of the group.

But the most ambiguous word is one that the Japanese have recently borrowed from English with a slight modification in its pronunciation. It is the word *rejā*, which means "leisure."

In English, leisure is leisure. In Japan, leisure means boredom, for the great majority of the working people simply do not know what do when they have a day off. That is why they are called "workaholics."

And the difference between most "workaholics" and some "money-worshippers" is that the former never make enough money to have a place to live in when they retire, and the latter go on accumulating huge amounts of it until they are so old that they cannot enjoy either money or *rejā*.

For example, an 86-year-old Japanese farmer, in a contribution to *Okane*, dated March 18, 1989, wrote about a friend of his who once told him :

"Life is money. I'm going to work and make money until the age of 70, and then enjoy it."

At the time he was in his twenties. At 30, at 40 and at 60 he told him exactly the same thing, and he accomplished his goal : he became a millionaire.

He met his friend again after a long time, when he was 75 or 76. He had a dejected look on his face, and did not seem to be in the best of health.

"How are you?"

"Not very well. I have lost my appetite, and I am bored to death."

"Why don't you try doing some kind of physical exercise?"

"Oh, no. I have stopped doing things that make me sweat."

He suggested that he should try *go*, a Japanese game played by two persons on a wooden square board with black and white flat round stones, or *bonsai*, which is the art of raising miniature potted trees. The answer was that *go* was boring and *bonsai* too troublesome.

"What about reading the newspaper?"

"Oh, no."

"What about watching television?"

"I am sick and tired of watching television every day from morning to night."

"Why don't you try travelling with your wife to Hawaii or Hong Kong?"

"We are too old for that sort of thing."

The contributor concluded by saying that his friend has reached his goal of making money by working until he was 70, but failed in his goal of enjoying it, and now he is just a living corpse.

The only comment I can make is that there seem to be many other living corpses in Japan, with the only difference that some of them have not even enough money to go on living as living corpses.

22

BILLIONAIRES? WHO AND HOW MANY?

When I first came to Japan, Western people were saying: "The Japanese are economic animals."

I never came across one who fitted that description. But as the Japanese themselves are now affirming in their letters to the *Asahi Shimbun*, there were "economic animals," even before I came here.

But were there many of them? I do not know.

A few years after I came to Japan, somebody whose name and nationality I have forgotten, in a report to the European Common Market wrote a sentence that became famous all over the world: "The Japanese are workaholics who live in rabbit hutches."

Although I found the epithet "workaholics" rather exaggerated, and the metaphorical expression "rabbit hutch" too sarcastic, it was true that they were working longer hours and much more conscientiously than Europeans, and that they were living in very small apartments or houses.

Were there any people who were not working at all? I do not know. But as the protagonist of a novel by Yasunari Kawabata is a *himajin*, which means "man of leisure" or "idler," there must also have been such people in real life. I never met one of them.

Were there people living in large and comfortable apartments or houses? Very few.

At present, Japan is an economic superpower. This is an axiomatic truth. And if you start from this premise and make a syllogism according to the rules that Aristotle established for logical reasoning, you will come to the conclusion that the great majority of people living and working in a country which is an economic superpower must be enjoying a comfortable life.

But Aristotle was Greek, and what was and is still logical in Greece and the rest of the world, is not necessarily logical in Japan.

And many Japanese tell you, and demonstrate with irrefutable arguments based on concrete cases, that although Japan is an economic superpower, the common people are not affluent at all. And as if that were not enough, they tell you that the increase of the affluence of the nation is directly proportional to the decrease of the affluence of the people.

And when you ask them if there are any people who are living off the fat of the land, they answer that there are very few of them.

The letters to the editor which I have read confirm what they say.

For example, a 37-year-old public servant, in a contribution to *Okane*, dated December 2, 1988, describes the life he is leading.

He says that he works day after day just in order to eke out a meager living. With the salary he is earning, far from saving, he will have to run into debt. On Sundays he is so tired, that in order to get rid of stress he lies down on the *tatami* mat and watches television. On television there are programs about gourmets and people who travel, and they make him feel as if he were one of them. But the illusion does not last long. On Sunday evening he begins to think that on the following morning he has to go back to work.

"If this is happiness," he says, "I don't want it. I prefer money, a lot of it. And that is what the people want : money."

Of course, not everybody is leading the same sad life, and there are other people who can afford the luxury of travelling. But not all of them are leading such a comfortable life as one might imagine.

For example, a 29-year-old housewife, in a letter dated November 5, 1988, explains how she manages to travel.

She says that she has a friend who is always complaining about her husband's salary. Her own husband is an employee of an important company, and is not earning much more. But her friend is always buying new clothes, new electrical appliances and a lot of toys for the children, while she has no car, eats cheap food and goes on using the same old electrical appliances until they are beyond repair. She buys clothes and toys at bargain sales, and borrows books from the library.

Thanks to such an economical life, the whole family can enjoy travelling all together.

23

THE BEST WAY TO UNDERSTAND JAPANESE SOCIETY

Japan used to be a country of avid readers, and the publishing business was one of the most booming in the world.

It still is. The only difference is that the reading matter has changed from literature, poetry, culture, science etc. to *manga* (comics), some of which are as big as encyclopedic dictionaries of more than one thousand pages, and an infinite number of books, newspapers, magazines, both weekly and monthly, and of course *manga*, about business, stock, investment, real estate and the like.

And when you turn over the pages of newspapers that in the past only contained news, you will find that a good deal of space is devoted to interminable lists of small numbers : the quotation of the Stock Exchange, Mutual Funds, etc.

The other day I got into conversation with a Japanese elderly man, whom I often meet on the train.

He is one of those Japanese who only use English when they are talking with a foreigner, even if they know that the foreigner they are talking to is not a native English speaker and understands Japanese.

He said with bitterness that Japan has become a country of readers who are not readers but "lookers," and of stockholders who are not stockholders but "candleholders."

I understood the pun about "lookers" of comics, but not the one about "candleholders." I just nodded, and refrained from asking for an explanation.

He told me that he was a philosophy professor, and that "when the Japanese were still Japanese," he had written two or three best-sellers about the infinite scheme of things.

I do not know if one of these days I will decide to devote my spare time to comics, but I am sure that I will never become a "candleholder" for two reasons : I do not like gambling, and I have no money.

But in a country where even junior high school students are taught the game, I am beginning to think that is a shame for a university professor not to try and learn it.

For example, a 73-year-old man, in a letter to the editor of the *Okane*, dated November 8, 1988, said that when NTT began to sell shares, his wife had a telephone call from their granddaughter, who is a junior high school student.

"Grandmother, won't you buy some NTT stock?"

She got the shock of her life. She had never even mentioned the word "stock."

"Buy stock? Why should I?"

"Our teacher taught us that if we buy stock, we'll be able to understand the mechanism of our society."

"Of course. Not only of Japan, but the whole world. I will think about it. But remember that the most important thing is to study hard."

This contributor concludes by saying that it is very sad to see that nowadays in Japan there are junior high schools where teachers are stimulating girls to become interested in buying and selling stock. But he adds that his way of thinking is probably too old-fashioned.

Yesterday I met the philosophy professor again, and asked him what he meant by "candleholders."

He explained to me that according to a recent study, only 20% of the common people who buy stock make profits. The rest are just holding a candle to the corporations, that is to say, helping the people who are exploiting them, or a candle to the devil, that is to say, to the politicians that have caused this "execrable stock mania," and the result is that they are holding a candle to the sun, that is to say, doing something which is getting them nowhere.

And then he added that although such Japanese stockholders are "candleholders," they can not hold a candle to American stockholders (?).

When we parted, my head was full of candles.

24

ALL ARE EQUAL, BUT SOME ARE MORE EQUAL THAN OTHERS

Mariko Sugawara, a counsellor at the Cabinet Secretariat, in an article which was published in the *Shizuoka Shimbun* on March 5, 1989, says that Japanese corporations are making huge investments overseas, and in Japan they are holding extravagant banquets at prohibitively expensive places day in and day out. On the other hand, the family budget of each of the individuals belonging to Japanese corporations is so meager that they have to struggle to make ends meet.

One of the reasons for this contradiction is the fact that the profits of the company are not proportional to the salaries, which are kept at a low level which is practically the same for all, and no difference is made between mere clerks and division chiefs.

But there is a great difference in the case of "expense accounts." For division chiefs live in large and comfortables *shataku*, can play golf at exclusive and expensive clubs and use luxury cars — and all of that is paid by the company.

This system is convenient both for the employers, who obtain the employees' loyalty by keeping them economically and psychologically dependent on them, and for the employees who can go to the best restaurants and golf clubs without paying any bills or any income taxes on such expenses.

The result of this system is the lack of independence on the part of the employee, the loss of the spirit of fair play, and the ideology that what is good for the company is good for the individual.

The employer does not pay taxes on these expenses, and the employees who enjoy and take advantage of them eat, drink and play golf in order to entertain customers and do business for the company.

The conclusion at which Mariko Sugawara arrives is that this system is the hotbed of affairs like the Recruit scandal, and that it is necessary to change it, by giving economical and psychological independence to employees through salaries according to their capacity and the profits of the company.

In a few words, this strange "egalitarianism," or "groupism" of people who work "for the company" is at the root of the incredible lack of affluence of the common people in an affluent nation. And perhaps there is some truth in the humorous remark made by a Japanese fellow who said that loyalty to the company is essentially the same thing as allegiance to the sovereign in feudal times.

Thanks to the explanation given by Mariko Sugawara, I learned something new about Japan and the Japanese : all is not gold that glitters, and not all gold-eating economic animals are wallowing in money.

And thanks to the Japanese philosophy professor who filled my head with candles when he was speaking about the people who instead of buying his books (or mine) are wasting it on stock, I understood that a syllogism is a syllogism not only in Greece and in any other Western country, but also in Japan.

He proved to me that I was wrong in conjecturing that Aristotle is turning in his grave, because what is happening in this country does not contradict his laws of formal logic : the syllogism about common people living and working in a country which is an economic superpower, and who are not leading a comfortable life, is a sophism, due to a gross error in the premise.

According to him, Aristotle would correct the premise "Japan is a country which is an economic superpower" to "Japan is a country which belongs to a few economically superpowerful rational animals."

25

THE ECONOMICALLY SUPERPOWERFUL SPECIMENS OF HOMO SAPIENS

Japanese corporations are investing billions and billions of dollars overseas, and there are some American economists who speculate that it will not be long before they buy at least three of the six continents.

They will change the way of life, working and housing conditions of their inhabitants, including the presidents, queens and kings of each country, and transform everybody, in a liberal and democratic way, into a docile, obedient and faithful member of a society of national consensus.

According to an article by Robert Neff and Paul Magnusson in *Business Week*, dated August 7, 1989—which my wife bought for me when I was correcting the manuscript of this book—House Majority Leader Richard A. Gephardt (D-Mo.), who ran a "faltering Presidential primary campaign on Japan and the trade deficit," is now pursuing the issue with more sophistication : he is studying Japanese!

An Englishman I met on a train told me that in his opinion, Gephardt is studying Japanese because he has a presentiment of what the future has in store for him and his fellow-countrymen : what used to be one of the Crown Colonies, will become part of the Japanese Economic Empire, and he will have to master the language of his landlord in order to get a discount on the rent, the *reikin* and so forth.

The Englishman went on to say that the Statue of Liberty will be given a new name : The Statue of the Geisha of the Group—unless the machos in the ruling party, who seem to be laboring under the illusion that women are the "weaker sex," have made a fatal mistake.

The purchase of the three continents will be possible thanks to the "magic power" of the yen, which is almost worthless at home and incredibly valuable overseas.

A 34-year-old Japanese housewife, in a contribution to *Okane*, dated January 7, 1989, after mentioning the purchase of an oil painting by Van Gogh, for which an enormous price was paid, says that in Australia and in a lot of other countries Japanese real estate companies are buying the best resort places for amounts of money which are incredibly high overseas, but not necessarily so in Japan. And the people of those countries are worried and angry at the increase in land prices—and the destruction of natural beauty which may be the result of such an invasion.

She is at present living in London. In Tokyo she was living in a small apartment with two rooms and a dining-kitchen, and sending her daughter to the kindegarten was a great burden for the family. When they went to London, they became what she calls a"Cinderella family," living in a large house with a garden, and two cars.

It is not clear from the letter whether her husband is an executive or a mere clerk of an important Japanese company. But as the salary is practically the same for all, I would not be surprised if he were a division chief.

What sounds incredible is the fact that for the family of a Japanese employee even sending a child to the kindergarten constitutes a considerable burden.

Still, the working people of Japan seem to be

resigned to such a situation, and until recently, they have considered themselves to be "middle-class people," and have accepted the "egalitarianism" and "loyalty to the company," which are required in return for life employment, *shataku*, free expense accounts etc. as the most natural things in the world. That is what has made of Japan such a great economic power, and the yen so strong.

In the Western world, working people have their own political party, which defends their interests. In Japan they have been relying on the Liberal-Democratic Party, which is in close alliance with the employers, and is only looking after the interest of their corporations.

Thanks to this alliance, and the psychological subjugation of the working class to it, the standard of life of people who in the past used to live in extreme poverty has risen, but not in proportion to the amount and quality of their work and the profits of the corporations for which they are working.

As a consequence of the increase of the cost of living, which bears no relation to the increase of salaries, life is becoming more and more difficult for the common people.

Corporations have increased the number of working hours, as a result of which the number of cases of death due to excessive work, lack of leisure, stress, and nervous exhaustion has also increased.

In a society where there is no fair play on the part of either the employer or the political party that only supports the employer, and strict obedience on the part of workers who do not seem to realize that they are treated like "robots," as a Japanese young man was saying the other day, it is logical that the only people who have become rich in the real meaning of the word are employers, politicians, and the people who have benefited from the policy of the goverment.

The gap between those who have and those who have not is becoming wider as time elapses. And the people who think they have are not so numerous as they used to be.

Japanese politicians of the ruling party, in their electoral speeches promise that they will do their best "for the people," but it is also logical that if they depend on the contribution of businessmen in order to carry on their political activity in the nation and within the party itself, they will do their best not for the people, but for the corporations that support them, their political party, or their own faction within the party—and of course, themselves as individuals.

26

"WELL-AND-FENCE" POLITICIANS

According to Japanese journalists and columnists, political activity in Japan has always cost a lot of money, but in the past it was not a business, although it was necessary to invest your own money, and you ran the risk of going into bankruptcy.

At present, they say that in most cases it is a business, and a very funny one.

In the first place, in order to start it you do not need money, but good connections, and once you have embarked on it, you may be sure that you will earn billions of yen, provided you choose the right political party for your career, and your only aspiration is making money.

In a few words, as a politician, you will never find yourself in a difficult economic situation : you will have a lot of chances of making a fortune with other people's money and absolutely no risks of losing yours.

That is why the political career in Japan is the most lucrative business in the world—unless you are an idealist, or a fool.

In the opinion of most Japanese, at present there are few idealists and no fools in the political world.

Among the politicians of the past, there were many idealists, and some of them went into bankruptcy for the only reason that they were too honest and did not choose the political career in order to make money. They were called *idobei seijika*, which means "well-and-fence politicians," that is to say, politicians who lost all their fortune and the house where they were living, except the well in the garden and the fence around it.

A 61-year-old housewife, in a contribution to *Okane*, dated December 17, 1988, wrote about her father, who was a typical "well-and-fence" politician.

When she was a child, her family owned so much land, that many people said that you could walk from her house to the railway station without treading on soil that belonged to somebody else. Although she adds that those who said that were exaggerating, one may assume that the railway station must have been very far from her house.

Her father engaged in politics, and little by little he lost almost all his fortune. When he retired, the only thing that was left was the house in which they were living.

To give an example of what the political activity meant to him and his family, she says that when her sister got married, they celebrated it with expensive wedding parties on three successive evenings. Her own wedding party was different as chalk from cheese.

After a brief reference to the Recruit affair, she concludes by saying that recently some young members of the Diet were complaining about the cost of their political activity, but she has not heard of anybody losing his fortune on account of it.

A 61-year-old man, in a letter dated March 4, 1989, as a "well-and-fence politician," gives the example of Aiichiro Fujiyama, who left financial activity in order to become a politician and ruined the fortune of the Fujiyama family.

He says that nowadays there are very few people who will think that he was an exemplary politician. On the contrary, he thinks that most people will probably say that what he did was foolish.

However, the expression *idobei seijika* can only be found in a big Japanese-Japanese dictionary, which means that it is as obsolete as a house with a well in the garden.

27

THOSE WHO HAVE, THOSE WHO HAVE NOT AND THOSE WHO THINK THEY HAVE

Japan has become an economic superpower thanks to hard work, low salaries, little social welfare, oppressive taxes, high cost of living, skyrocketing land prices, austerity, sacrifice, self-discipline, obedience, patience and resignation.

The gap between the "haves" and the "have-nots" is rapidly increasing. If you have not, by working hard the only thing you can hope for is to have enough to delude yourself into thinking that you have.

In the opinion of a Japanese who has read *The Divine Comedy*, for young men entering a company they should put this sign on the door: "Ye who enter here, abandon all hope of buying your own home."

Why have land prices increased to such levels?

Nobody knows. There is a theory that it was due to a speculation made by politicians with the object of filling more bushes and more safes with stacks of bills, or a confabulation between them and employers of big corporations in order to transform the whole country into a conglomerate of *shataku*, except for a few luxurious residential districts for themselves.

In any case, in this country, where nobody knows what has happened, what is happening and what will happen, the ones who have benefited most from this mysterious increase are land-owners.

A 52-year-old housewife, in a letter to the editor of *Okane*, dated September 20, 1988, wrote about the first *tochi narikin*, which means "land-owning nouveaux riches."

About 23 years ago, when the economic boom began, farms were transformed into residential districts, and straw-thatched houses became luxurious residences.

Farmers began to compete with one another in showing off their recently acquired wealth by adorning their gardens with stones. If one of them was told that another farmer had bought a given number of tons of stones, he ordered double the amount.

There were two types of *tochi narikin* : those who had come to buy land after the war, and local farmers. The latter, even after selling part of their land and building fine houses, went on living and dressing like farmers.

Among the farmers who sold or bought, the ones who had foresight to wait until the right moment, became the richest of all. And the big buildings and supermarkets which soar on what used to be farms or empty plots of land are the tangible proof of their wisdom.

But if you draw the conclusion that thanks to the increase of land prices, Japanese who own a house have nothing to worry about, you will be wrong. In a country like Japan, where the strangest things happen, there are people who are in trouble just because of the increase in the value of the land where their houses are built.

The first time I heard of it was when I read a letter which a 49-year-old housewife contributed to *Okane* on October 5, 1988.

She lives in what used to be a desolate place between Shinjuku and Nakano. Due to the increase in land prices in the last four or five years, day and night she is visited by real estate agents asking her to sell them the house, in a wheedling or a threatening voice.

She is a bundle of nerves. Her mother-in-law is almost 80 years old, and the house belongs to her. What is going to happen when she dies?

She went to the tax counsellor, and was told that inheritance taxes will amount to nearly ¥100,000,000, which is an enormous sum for them. Her husband is a common employee. If they sell that small piece of land where will they go? And if they don't, they will not be able to pay the inheritance taxes.

"Why has Japan has become such a strange country?" she wonders, when she thinks about their plight.

I was told that inheritance taxes have also been increased so much, that if you have a small house, your children will be able to pay them somehow. But not your grandchildren. And in the end, it will become the property of the Government. And the Government will become more and more economically powerful.

28

WHAT IS ONE HUNDRED MILLION YEN?

When I read what a 40-year-old housewife wrote in a contribution to *Okane*, dated October 7, 1988, about the price of two houses that were built in the vicinity of her own, I was not so surprised as she seems to be.

Both of them were modern two-story houses, had a total floor area of 30 *tsubo* (about a hundred square meters), and the space between them was less than 30 centimeters. The price was ¥189,000,000.

"Nearly 200,000,000 for such houses!" she thought. "What kind of people are going to buy them?"

Six months elapsed, and the houses were still vacant. One day she looked at the ad of the real estate company which was selling them, and was astonished to see that the price had been lowered to ¥148,000,000.

"In six months a reduction of ¥40,000,000!" she exclaimed.

What was the real value of the house? How had the initial price of ¥189,000,000 been calculated? With a reduction of ¥40,000,000 would they still make a profit or sustain a great loss?

¥40,000,000! ¥40,000,000 is a fabulous amount of money for the common people, who cannot afford to pay it even after working all their life. And to think that it was a mere reduction owing to the fact they could not wait more than six months in order to find a buyer!

She concludes by saying that prices of houses in Japan are beyond her comprehension. And she is Japanese.

But now it has become common knowledge that such an amount of money is a pittance for people like a prime minister who receives ¥200,000,000 as a political contribution "without his knowledge," and for those people who for some mysterious reasons hide the same sum of money in a bush, or those who put it into a safe and forget all about it not for six months, but for about 20 years, until the safe is found among the garbage, where it was discarded because it was too old.

Therefore, it is not difficult to imagine who

will buy such houses, although nobody will ever know how and where they got the money from.

But what is much more difficult to understand, at least for Westerners, is why the working people do not organize their own political party, in order to get such salaries as will allow them to live decently and be able, within a reasonable period of time, to buy their own apartment or house.

Mariko Sugiwara says that the only way of out the situation in which the working people find themselves at present, is to establish fair play in the distribution of profits and eliminate excessive dependence on the company.

It is hard to believe that working people have no ambition for economic independence. But do they want, or feel the need for psychological independence from the company? That is the question.

29

"WORKER BEES" OR "WORKAHOLICS?"

Whether most Japanese people are "work-aholics," as they are called by foreigners, or "worker bees," as they often call themselves, is a moot question. What is beyond doubt is the fact that they work more than anybody else in the world, and according to the results of a poll which was conducted by the Prime Minister's Office in November 1988, in spite of the movement in favor of a five-day week and longer holidays, they seem to enjoy work much more than leisure.

A 33-year-old teacher, in a letter to the editor of *Okane*, dated March 10, 1989, expressed the opinion that even if the goal of reducing working hours were accomplished, there would be a lot of Japanese who would not know what to do in their free time, and giving them leisure would be "casting pearls before the swine."

The poll seems to confirm what he says, although it shows a slight increase in the number of working people who would like to have more free time, in comparison with the results of the poll conducted three years ago.

To the question about whether they feel satisfied with the free time they have, 52.1% replied "Yes," and 46.6% "No."

To the question about their opinion as regards work and leisure, approximately 40% replied that both work and leisure are equally important, which was more or less the same percentage as 3 years ago.

29% replied that work is more important than leisure, and that the object of free time is to rest in order to be able to go on working, a percentage that was slightly lower.

Only 11.1% answered that leisure is more important than work, and that the object of work is to earn money in order to be able to enjoy life and leisure, a percentage slightly higher than 3 years ago.

Approximately 50% of those who replied that work and leisure are equally important, are in their twenties, and 42.4% of those who replied that work is more important than leisure are in their fifties.

The husband of a 25-year-old housewife, who

wrote a letter to the editor of *Okane*, dated April 8, 1989, is a typical example of the younger generation who think that family life and leisure are very important.

Although he received many offers from first-class corporations, he was very careful in his selection. After rejecting most of the offers, there were only two companies left : one was an important publishing industry and the other a large company connected with the oil business. In the case of the former, the main advantage was that after working for two consecutive years he would get a yearly income of ¥5,000,000. In the case of the latter, the salary was even lower than usual.

"Of course, he will enter the publishing company," she thought. To her surprise, he decided to enter the company connected with the oil business.

"In the publishing company they give you the chance of earning more, but you have to work so hard and so many hours, that you are so busy that you can't spend either money or time with your family. So, what are you working for?" he said. "In the other company they give you a *shataku* and two days off a week."

She says that they do not think that free time is absolutely the most important thing in life, but they are a happy family enjoying all the leisure they can get, and although they are not leading a life of comfort and luxury, they are not so poor as to envy anybody. And they do not have to fear *karōshi*, which means "death from overwork."

After reading this letter, I came across an article about what happens to the families of working people who die from *karōshi*. And I understood why that Japanese told me that if I went on reading Japanese newspapers, I would find articles that would remind me of the workmen who built the Pyramid of Cheops.

30

WORKING FOR THE PROSPERITY OF THE COMPANY AND...

Generally speaking, in the Western industrialized countries, most working people consider work as a means to an end : to be able to enjoy life as much as possible. And the factory or the office is merely the place where they have to work in order to obtain the necessary money which will allow them to achieve a decent standard of life.

In order to get the best salary they can, they have labor unions that defend their interests, and when they find it necessary to fight against the employers, they go on strike. And there are all kinds of strikes : general strikes, legal and illegal strikes, official and unofficial strikes, short and prolonged strikes, "lights out" strikes, sporadic strikes, "go slow" strikes, "leave of absence" strikes, "paralysis strikes," sit-down strikes, "stay-in" strikes, "sympathy strikes," etc., etc.

At least in the last few years, in Japan you never hear about any strikes, although everybody is complaining about the cost of living which is the highest in the world, and goes on rising even for imported goods in spite of the strength of the yen. And you wonder whether there are any labor unions at all.

In the opinion of a Japanese friend of mine, the reason for the complete psychological subjugation of Japanese working people lies in the fact that work is considered the chief end in life. Life without work is not considered worth living, and a Japanese out of the company where he is working, or overworking, feels like a fish out of water.

A Japanese can do without leisure and family life, but not without the company. The company is his world, and he only feels comfortable when he is on the job.

That is why companies obtain from working men a loyalty which is really unique.

A 41-year-old housewife, in a letter to the editor of *Okane*, dated March 2, 1989, said she was offered the opportunity of doing part-time work in a company, and accepted it without first consulting with her husband.

She taught her child how to use the electric kitchen and the washing machine, and went happily to her work. But after a week or two, she noticed that her husband looked gloomy and avoided speaking to her as though he were very angry at her.

After three weeks, he stopped speaking to her, and began to sleep in another bed. She was surprised and worried, and told a friend of hers what was happening.

"Which is more important for you, money or your husband? If you don't want to lose your husband, what you have to do is stop working."

She decided to follow her friend's advice, and after telling her employer a lie about the impossibility of leaving her child alone, she left the company, after working for a month.

After she had stopped working, her husband wrote her a long letter, in which he told her that when he was a child his mother was working, and he spent a miserable childhood in the loneliness of his house. He did not want his child to go through the same experience, and if more money was necessary, he would try and do his best to earn it himself.

On March 28, 1989, a 58-year-old housewife who had read her letter to the editor, wrote about it, and asked the "lady who had received the long letter" whether she had reflected about the inconvenience that she had caused by lying and leaving the company after only one month's work.

One month is barely enough to give the necessary training to a new employee, and when somebody like her suddenly says good-bye like that, all the strenuous efforts made in order to give the best possible training end in a waste of time—and money, for the company has to spend a lot of it on ads which are very expensive.

After criticizing her attitude, she goes on to speak about herself. She says that before she decided to work, she consulted many times with her husband, and he agreed on condition that she would never say, either at the company or at home, the words "I am tired."

She has been working for 8 years, and stresses the fact that she has always been working for the same company.

When I read these two letters, I reacted in exactly the same way as most of my readers will. But not my wife.

Of course, she sympathized with both the husband who wrote the long letter, and the wife who stopped working. But when she read the second letter, in which the housewife who was doing part-time work for the company spoke as if she were the employer and defending her own interests, the kind of surprise that she expressed was different from mine.

She stood agape for a moment, and then exclaimed :

"This lady is exactly like my father!"

It was my turn to stand agape. For the first time I realized that her father was the Western version of a Japanese employee.

He devoted all his life to an insurance company, and loved his work so much, that he used to go to the office even on Sundays whenever he felt it was necessary to do so.

The company was like an extension of his home. He looked after its interests as if they were his own, was incredibly proud of it, and always spoke about it as if it were the best company in the world.

"Are you sure there were no Japanese among his ancestors?" I asked my wife.

It is true that in the Western world there are not many employees like my father-in-law, and I could not contradict a Japanese who said that as regards loyalty to the company, what is the exception in the West is the rule in Japan.

But as regards the way loyalty to the company is rewarded, what in the West is the rule is the exception in Japan.

According to an article which appeared in the *Asahi Evening News* on July 7, 1989, the number of victims of *karōshi* among stressed-out working people, from executives to maintenance workers, is growing at an alarming rate. And families of the victims get little, if any compensation for the loss of a breadwinner.

In over 95 percent of the cases, the government ruled against paying workman's compensation because it is difficult to prove overwork was the cause of death.

But as a Japanese employee was telling me the other day, the politicians in the government who have no knowledge of the astronomical amounts of money their secretaries receive from corporations, probably have no knowledge, either, of the fact that Japanese are on the job an average 2,150 hours a year, compared with 1,924 hours in the United States and 1,665 hours in West Germany, according to the Labor Ministry. And that some firms require employees to work up to 3,000 hours per year, according to a survey by the government-affiliated Leisure Development Center.

"What's strange about it?" he said, when I looked at him in utter astonishment. "Our politicians are too busy counting their stacks of

¥10,000 bills to have any time to glance over the results of polls and surveys about such matters."

But these politicians leaped out of the pan of Recruit into the fire of the consumption tax — and the geisha scandal.

As a woman, my wife understands the eternal feminine power much better than overconfident machos do, and predicted that women would teach them a lesson they would never forget.

"Though the Mills of Women grind slowly, yet they grind exceeding small," quoth she.

She was right. On July 23, 1989, the Liberal-Democratic Party suffered a humiliating defeat in the Upper House election, and the single-party hegemony of Japan's macho politicians suddenly collapsed.

I hope that the beautiful Mills of the Women of the Land of the Rising Sun will grind so small that I may be able to go back to my ivory tower.

DOMENICO LAGANA, an Italian Japanologist, is a professor
at Hosei University and author of many books in Japanese.

『ラガナ一家のニッポン日記』,文藝春秋・角川文庫
『続ラガナ一家のニッポン日記』,文藝春秋・角川文庫
『日本語とわたし』,文藝春秋
『ラガナの文章修業』,講談社
対談集『紅毛碧眼日本語談義』,小学館
『ビアンカネラ物語』,河出書房新社
『ラガナのにっぽん子育て日記』,河出書房新社
『これは日本語か』,河出書房新社
etc.

YOHAN LOTUS BOOKS

NON-FICTION

FICTION